STECK-VAUGHN

Comprehension Skills
INFERENCE
LEVEL
F

STECK-VAUGHN
C O M P A N Y
A Subsidiary of National Education Corporation

Executive Editor:	Diane Sharpe
Project Editor:	Melinda Veatch
Design Coordinator:	Sharon Golden
Project Design:	Howard Adkins Communications
Cover Illustration:	Rhonda Childress
Photographs:	©Focus on Sports

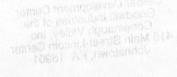

ISBN 0-8114-7859-9

7 8 9 10 VP 01 00 99 98

Making an inference means making a guess. You can make this guess by putting together what you know and what you read. In this book you will make inferences about stories.

You make inferences all the time. Look at the picture. Have you ever won an important game? Did you feel happy or excited? How do you think the players in this picture feel? What helped you make this inference?

What Is an Inference?

An inference is a guess you make after thinking about what you already know. For example, suppose you plan to go to the beach. From what you know about beaches, you might infer that the beach is covered with sand and the sun is shining.

An author does not write every detail in a story. If every detail were included, stories would be long and boring, and the main point would be lost. As you read, the writer expects you to fill in missing details from your own experiences. Suppose you read, "Sabrina went to the library." The writer does not have to tell you the specifics about what a library is. You already know it is a place where people go when they want to borrow books. You might infer that there are tables and chairs where people can sit and read books and magazines. People who have library cards may check out books and other materials and take them home. By filling in these missing details, you can infer that Sabrina went to the library to check out books. You can make this inference based on what you know.

Try It!

Read this story about blacksmiths, and then think about the facts.

◆

> There were many blacksmiths in colonial America. Blacksmiths spent long hours hammering the hot iron used to make tools. They made horseshoes, axes, hoes, plow blades, kettles, and pots for the townspeople. Blacksmiths who lived near shipyards made anchors, rudder irons, and tools for ships.

What inference can you make about blacksmiths? Write an inference on the line below.

You might have written something such as "Blacksmiths made most of the important tools in colonial America." You can make these inferences by putting together the facts in the story and what you already know.

Using What You Know

This book asks you to make inferences. Read the paragraphs on this page. Then make an inference based on what you've read and what you know. Write an inference on the line below each paragraph.

It was the final day of school. All the books and supplies had been turned in, and everyone was attending the honors and awards assembly. This had been my best year at school. During the assembly I was to receive three ribbons for track and field along with awards for mathematics and perfect attendance. I smiled broadly as I walked up onto the stage to accept my awards.

I felt _____.

It was my turn at bat. This was the moment I had been dreading. The ball whizzed past me three times. I swung three times without coming close to hitting the ball. When the umpire yelled "Strike three!", I walked back into the dugout with my head down.

I was _____.

I love to read biographies of sports heroes, and I had just checked a book out of the library about Michael Jordan. I was reading it when Mom asked me to go outside and watch my little sister. *I'll go in a minute*, I thought as I turned to the next page.

Next I _____.

I had been waiting eagerly for my report card. I had been trying for six weeks to improve my grades. If they were better this time, I would be on the honor roll. The teacher smiled as she handed me the report card. "Congratulations," she said.

I felt _____.

Practice Making Inferences

Read each story, and then read the statements that follow. Some of the statements are facts. They can be found in the story. Other statements are inferences. Decide whether each statement is a fact or an inference. The first one has been done for you.

◆

Rebecca's mother woke her up at 6:30. "I have to leave early for work this morning," she said. "Please get up and start dressing so you'll be ready when the bus comes." Rebecca turned over and pulled the pillow over her head.

Fact	Inference	
○	●	**1. A.** Rebecca went back to sleep.
●	○	**B.** Rebecca's mother woke her up.
○	●	**C.** Rebecca missed the bus.
○	●	**D.** Rebecca wasn't ready to get up.

The first sentence of the story says that Rebecca's mother woke her, so we know that **B** is a fact. You can guess that Rebecca went back to sleep, but it isn't stated in the story, so **A** is an inference. You can also guess that Rebecca missed the bus and that she wasn't ready to get up, but neither of these is stated in the story. Therefore, **C** and **D** are also inferences.

◆

Every summer sea turtles come to the remote beaches near Boca Raton, Florida. With their large front flippers, the female turtles dig large pits in the sand and then deposit perfectly round, white eggs. The eggs have leathery shells. The female turtle pushes sand over the eggs, and then she crawls back into the ocean. Scientists take many groups of people to see the sea turtles laying their eggs.

Fact	Inference	
○	○	**2. A.** Sea turtles dig large pits in the sand.
○	○	**B.** Many people are interested in the sea turtles.
○	○	**C.** The mother turtle does not stay with the eggs.
○	○	**D.** The eggs have leathery shells.

To check your answers, turn to page 62.

How to Use This Book

Read the stories in this book, and answer the questions after each story. You can check your answers yourself. If you wish, tear out pages 59 through 62, and find the unit you want to check. Fold the answer page on the dotted line to show the correct unit, and line it up with the answers you wrote. Write the number of correct answers in the score box at the top of each answer page.

You can have fun making inferences. Turn to pages 56 through 58 and work through "Think and Apply."

Remember

In this book you are asked to find facts and make inferences. Read each story, and then read the statements that follow the story. Which of these statements can you find in the story? These are facts. Which statements can you infer by thinking about what you've read and what you know? These are inferences.

Hints for Better Reading

◆ As you read keep in mind the difference between facts and inferences.

◆ Think about the facts in the story, and think about what you already know. Make an inference by putting together what you know and what you've read.

Challenge Yourself

Read each story. Mark your answers. Then write one more inference you can make about each story.

1. The ancient Greeks made up stories to explain their world. They thought that many gods and goddesses controlled the universe. The greatest Greek god was Zeus, who controlled the weather. When a storm raged with thunder and lightning, Zeus was at work. The Greeks believed that the natural world was alive and that it should be treated with respect.

2. When people began to grow crops, they needed to know when to plant their seeds. They noticed that the best time to plant came at the same time each year. The early Egyptians counted the number of full moons between planting times. The times between moons were called months of the year. The Egyptians then noticed a bright star in the sky at planting time. They counted 365 days between the appearances of this star. Then they divided these days by 12 months to invent the first year.

3. El Santo was a famous fellow in Mexico. He was successful as a wrestler. But he was a top movie star, too. In his movies he played a masked wrestler who helped catch criminals and monsters. His best film was *The Mummies of Guanajuato*. El Santo died in 1984.

4. Charlene awoke with a shriek. Her pajamas were soaked with sweat, and she could feel herself trembling inside. The night was dark and still, and the furniture in her room loomed like shadowy monsters. Charlene closed her eyes and tried to fall asleep again. But the night was too quiet, and her eyes popped open. Suddenly Charlene heard a scratching noise at her window, and she buried her head under her pillow.

5. Long ago, people did not really understand the cause of disease. So when they were sick, they tried any cure they could think of. Surprisingly this early medicine used some treatments that are still used today. These include herb cures and the use of heat and cold for body aches.

Fact	Inference		
○	○	**1.**	**A.** The Greeks did not understand science.
○	○		**B.** The Greeks thought Zeus controlled the weather.
○	○		**C.** The greatest Greek god was Zeus.
○	○		**D.** The Greeks thought Zeus was powerful.

Fact	Inference		
○	○	**2.**	**A.** Egyptians invented the first calendar.
○	○		**B.** The word *month* comes from the word *moon*.
○	○		**C.** The Egyptians were farmers.
○	○		**D.** The Egyptians counted days by the moon and stars.

Fact	Inference		
○	○	**3.**	**A.** The masked wrestler performed good deeds.
○	○		**B.** El Santo was a successful wrestler.
○	○		**C.** The Mexican people like wrestling.
○	○		**D.** El Santo died in 1984.

Fact	Inference		
○	○	**4.**	**A.** Charlene was scared.
○	○		**B.** A nightmare awoke Charlene.
○	○		**C.** Charlene's pajamas were soaked.
○	○		**D.** The night was quiet.

Fact	Inference		
○	○	**5.**	**A.** Long ago, people didn't understand disease.
○	○		**B.** Herbs were used in early medicine.
○	○		**C.** Long ago, people didn't have modern drugs.
○	○		**D.** Some early medical practices were helpful.

1. Over five thousand Mexican troops waited outside the Alamo to storm the walls. Only 180 Texans remained inside to defend the place. William Travis told his men that if they stayed to fight, they would likely die. Then he drew a line in the dirt with his sword and told those willing to stay to cross the line. All but one man stepped across.

2. The Trojan War had been fought between the Greeks and the Trojans for ten years. Then the Greek leader Odysseus ordered that a great wooden horse be built. When it was finished, many Greek soldiers climbed inside. The horse was left just outside the Trojan city of Troy. The Trojans thought it was a gift of peace from the Greeks, so they dragged it inside the walls of the city. That night as the Trojans slept, the Greeks streamed out of the horse to defeat the city.

3. Lucy Stone was an unusual woman in many ways. She graduated from college in the 1840s. Stone was the first woman in Massachusetts to do this. She also fought hard to end slavery. And when she married, she would not take her husband's last name. Lucy Stone became the first woman in the United States to keep her own name after marriage.

4. Over the years Jason and his dog Flash had shared many good times and great adventures. They played together, and sometimes they even slept together. But Flash got old, and his eyesight and hearing began to fade. He even started snapping at children, so Jason knew the time had come to put Flash to sleep. Although the idea of taking Flash to the vet made Jason very sad, he knew it was for the best.

5. Most football games last longer than 60 minutes. Games are divided into 4, 15-minute quarters. But the action in the game does not go on all that time. In fact the ball is in play only about 15 minutes of every game.

Fact	Inference	
◯	◯	**1. A.** The men in the Alamo had little chance to win.
◯	◯	**B.** William Travis drew a line in the dirt.
◯	◯	**C.** Five thousand Mexican troops waited outside.
◯	◯	**D.** The Texans were willing to die.

Fact	Inference	
◯	◯	**2. A.** Odysseus wanted to trick the Trojans.
◯	◯	**B.** The Trojans were caught by surprise.
◯	◯	**C.** Odysseus was a clever soldier.
◯	◯	**D.** The Trojan War lasted ten years.

Fact	Inference	
◯	◯	**3. A.** Lucy Stone went to college.
◯	◯	**B.** Few women went to college in the 1840s.
◯	◯	**C.** Lucy Stone felt that slavery was unjust.
◯	◯	**D.** Most married women took their husband's last name.

Fact	Inference	
◯	◯	**4. A.** Jason loves his dog Flash.
◯	◯	**B.** Sometimes Jason slept with Flash.
◯	◯	**C.** Flash's eyesight and hearing were fading.
◯	◯	**D.** Flash snapped at children.

Fact	Inference	
◯	◯	**5. A.** Football games have 4 quarters.
◯	◯	**B.** Each quarter is 15 minutes long.
◯	◯	**C.** The game stops and starts many times.
◯	◯	**D.** Football games last longer than one hour.

1. The construction of the Tower of Pisa began in 1174. But the builders made a big mistake. They built the foundation in sand, and sand shifts frequently. Over the years the tower started to lean. It now is more than 16 feet out of line.

2. Men and women button their clothes differently. There is a good reason for this difference. Buttons were first used to fasten clothes over 700 years ago. Buttons were expensive then, and only rich people could buy them. Most men are right-handed, so men's clothes were made to be buttoned easily by right-handed men. In those days most rich women were dressed by their right-handed servants. The servants faced the women to button their clothes. So women's clothes had buttons on the left so they could be buttoned easily by the servants.

3. Rebecca tossed and turned in her bed, unable to sleep. Her head hurt, and her stomach churned. She had cheated on a mathematics test that afternoon, and now she couldn't stop thinking about it.

4. Rodney bragged to his friends that he could find his way around anywhere. One day, though, Rodney was delivering pizza in a strange part of town. Though he searched for half an hour, he could not locate the address. Finally he had to stop to ask for directions. His face turned red, and he stuttered as he asked how to find the place.

5. The Civil War ended in 1865. The two opposing generals, Ulysses S. Grant and Robert E. Lee, met to discuss the terms of surrender. The site was a small town in Virginia called Appomattox Courthouse. The meeting was quiet and short, and they soon agreed to the terms. Afterward Grant said he was not overjoyed by the end of the war. Instead Grant felt sad Lee had lost. Grant respected Lee as a man who fought bravely for a cause he believed in.

Fact	Inference		
◯	◯	**1.** **A.**	Modern builders don't build on sand.
◯	◯	**B.**	The shifting sand caused the tower to lean.
◯	◯	**C.**	Construction of the tower began in 1174.
◯	◯	**D.**	The tower now leans more than 16 feet.

Fact	Inference		
◯	◯	**2.** **A.**	Buttons were first used over 700 years ago.
◯	◯	**B.**	At first buttons were expensive.
◯	◯	**C.**	Rich men dressed themselves.
◯	◯	**D.**	Most rich women were dressed by servants.

Fact	Inference		
◯	◯	**3.** **A.**	Rebecca cheated on a test.
◯	◯	**B.**	She felt guilty about cheating.
◯	◯	**C.**	Mathematics isn't easy for Rebecca.
◯	◯	**D.**	Rebecca wished she had not cheated.

Fact	Inference		
◯	◯	**4.** **A.**	Rodney didn't have a city map.
◯	◯	**B.**	Asking for directions embarrassed Rodney.
◯	◯	**C.**	Rodney delivered pizzas.
◯	◯	**D.**	Rodney searched for half an hour.

Fact	Inference		
◯	◯	**5.** **A.**	The Civil War ended in 1865.
◯	◯	**B.**	Lee felt the terms were fair.
◯	◯	**C.**	Lee and Grant met in Virginia.
◯	◯	**D.**	Grant felt sad that Lee had lost.

1. One Greek legend tells that at first fire belonged only to the gods on Mount Olympus. But down on Earth, Prometheus had created people from soil and water. He wanted to give his creations a special gift, so he entered heaven and stole some fire from the blazing sun. He returned to Earth and gave the fire to the people. Then they could cook, keep warm, and have light. They could also forge tools and weapons to make their lives easier.

2. Ludwig van Beethoven was one of the world's greatest composers. He wanted to play the piano, but as a young man he began to go deaf. So he turned to writing music. In fact much of his greatest music was written when he was totally deaf.

3. The young man wouldn't listen to anyone. He was too sure of himself and felt he could handle any situation. Others had warned him not to camp alone in the freezing weather, but he did not listen to them. So when he fell into icy water and could not build a fire to warm himself, no one was there to help him.

4. Dr. James Barry led a very strange life. He was a doctor in the British army. In the 1800s he rose to the top medical position in the army. But after he died, it was learned that Dr. Barry was really a woman! She had spent her whole medical career disguised as a man. In fact she had even given birth to a child, and yet her secret remained unknown.

5. Angela did not like to go to the park anymore. She used to spend her springtime afternoons there, enjoying the flowers and the fresh air. But now she saw more and more old people in the park, sitting alone on the benches. They seemed so sad and lonely that Angela wished she never had to grow old.

Fact	Inference		
○	○	**1.** **A.**	Prometheus brought fire to Earth.
○	○	**B.**	At first people did not have weapons.
○	○	**C.**	Mount Olympus was in heaven.
○	○	**D.**	Prometheus cared about his creations.

Fact	Inference		
○	○	**2.** **A.**	Beethoven began to go deaf as a young man.
○	○	**B.**	The piano was his favorite instrument.
○	○	**C.**	Beethoven was a great composer.
○	○	**D.**	He eventually became totally deaf.

Fact	Inference		
○	○	**3.** **A.**	The young man wouldn't listen to anyone.
○	○	**B.**	Others had warned him about camping alone.
○	○	**C.**	The man's stubbornness got him in trouble.
○	○	**D.**	The young man fell into icy water.

Fact	Inference		
○	○	**4.** **A.**	Others did not suspect Barry was a woman.
○	○	**B.**	Dr. Barry served in the British army.
○	○	**C.**	James Barry was a good doctor.
○	○	**D.**	In the 1880s women couldn't be in the army.

Fact	Inference		
○	○	**5.** **A.**	The old people make Angela feel uneasy.
○	○	**B.**	Angela enjoyed the flowers and fresh air.
○	○	**C.**	The old people seemed sad and lonely.
○	○	**D.**	Angela is afraid of growing old.

1. In 1830 Joseph Palmer was thrown in jail in Massachusetts. His crime was not a serious one. He simply tried to keep some men from shaving off his beard. Most American men at that time did not wear beards, so Palmer, with his flowing beard, was regarded as a crazy man. Four men attacked Palmer and tried to shave him. Palmer fought back and was put in jail for fighting. Over a year later, Palmer was finally released, still wearing his beard.

2. Wherever Edna went she took her lucky charm. She felt uncomfortable anytime she misplaced it. If she won a tennis match or did well on a test, Edna gave credit to her lucky charm. Her friends told her she did well because of her own talents, but Edna chose not to believe them.

3. The American Revolution was not going well. Supplies were running low, and the soldiers were starting to grumble. General George Washington chose a site in Valley Forge, Pennsylvania, where his army would spend the winter. The weather was quite cold, and food was scarce. Washington feared his men would not survive the severe conditions. But they did, and soon they won the war.

4. Albert stormed into his apartment and threw down his lunchbox. He had just lost his job. Albert had worked for the same company for over ten years. But today he had been informed that he was no longer needed. Albert didn't know what he would do now.

5. Caroline von Roeder left Germany in the 1830s. She was moving to Texas with her family. They thought that Texas would be a paradise and that they would have plenty of free time for hunting and fishing. Caroline brought along her piano and her favorite books. But when she and her family arrived in Texas, they were shocked. They found a rough land full of rough people. Instead of a life of leisure, they found a life of work and hardship.

Fact	Inference		
○	○	**1.**	**A.** Joseph Palmer was jailed in Massachusetts.
○	○		**B.** Four men attacked Joseph Palmer.
○	○		**C.** The four men did not like Palmer's beard.
○	○		**D.** Palmer stood up for his rights.

Fact	Inference		
○	○	**2.**	**A.** Edna had a lucky charm.
○	○		**B.** The lucky charm was important to Edna.
○	○		**C.** Edna did not believe in her abilities.
○	○		**D.** Her friends didn't believe in the charm.

Fact	Inference		
○	○	**3.**	**A.** George Washington was a general.
○	○		**B.** Valley Forge is in Pennsylvania.
○	○		**C.** The weather at Valley Forge was cold.
○	○		**D.** The lack of supplies upset the soldiers.

Fact	Inference		
○	○	**4.**	**A.** Albert threw down his lunchbox.
○	○		**B.** Albert's job had lasted over ten years.
○	○		**C.** Losing his job made Albert upset.
○	○		**D.** Albert lived in an apartment.

Fact	Inference		
○	○	**5.**	**A.** Caroline moved from Germany.
○	○		**B.** Caroline thought life in Germany was difficult.
○	○		**C.** Caroline brought her piano.
○	○		**D.** Her family had never been to Texas before.

1. Hercules was the strongest man in the world. His father was Zeus, king of the Greek gods. But Hera, the wife of Zeus, did not like Hercules, and she made him go mad. While mad, Hercules killed his family. As punishment for his crime, Hercules had to perform 12 labors. These tasks were nearly impossible, but Hercules finished them all. Finally his crime was pardoned.

2. Iwo Jima was the site of an important battle in World War II. American troops attacked the Japanese base on that island. The fight raged on for days, and losses were heavy on both sides. But at last the American troops triumphed. To honor the victory, a group of men raised an American flag on the island. One of these men was Ira Hayes, a member of the Native American Pima tribe.

3. Linda's summer vacation had seemed to drag on and on. The drive through South Dakota had been hot and boring. Then suddenly she saw the mountain with the four large faces carved in it, and her feeling changed quickly. When Linda looked up at Mount Rushmore, she was filled with awe and pride.

4. Joe's mother had told him that the cowboy would probably leave one day, but Joe did not want to believe her. Instead day by day his friendship with the old cowboy had grown stronger. Joe liked the way the cowboy mounted his horse and swung a lasso. He liked to listen as the cowboy told tales of cattle drives and stampedes. Then one day the old cowboy was gone, and Joe went off to the top of a hill to be alone.

5. One day Percy Spencer was working with microwave signals. In his pocket he had a candy bar for a snack. But Spencer soon noticed that he had a mess in his pocket. The signals had melted the candy bar. His accident led to the invention of the microwave oven.

Fact	Inference		
○	○	**1.**	**A.** Hercules was a strong man.
○	○		**B.** Zeus was the father of Hercules.
○	○		**C.** Hercules struggled to complete his labors.
○	○		**D.** Hera did not like Hercules.

Fact	Inference		
○	○	**2.**	**A.** Iwo Jima is an island.
○	○		**B.** The Americans were proud of their victory.
○	○		**C.** Ira Hayes was an American soldier.
○	○		**D.** American troops attacked Iwo Jima.

Fact	Inference		
○	○	**3.**	**A.** Linda didn't like her summer vacation.
○	○		**B.** The drive through South Dakota was hot.
○	○		**C.** Linda was excited when she saw Mount Rushmore.
○	○		**D.** Visiting Mount Rushmore made her feel better.

Fact	Inference		
○	○	**4.**	**A.** Joe hoped the cowboy would never leave.
○	○		**B.** The old cowboy could swing a lasso.
○	○		**C.** Joe was sad when the cowboy left.
○	○		**D.** The cowboy told stories about cattle drives.

Fact	Inference		
○	○	**5.**	**A.** Spencer worked with microwave signals.
○	○		**B.** Spencer was surprised to find the mess.
○	○		**C.** Microwave signals melted the candy bar.
○	○		**D.** Spencer did not get to eat his snack.

1. John Milton was one of England's greatest poets, but at the age of 44 he went blind. Since Milton could no longer write, he had to tell his poems to his daughter, who wrote them down. This method was slow and tiring. Milton's greatest poem, *Paradise Lost*, was long and took many months to complete.

2. Mary worked as a cook in a cafe. One day she got the great idea to cook the world's largest pancake. For days she worked to build a giant frying pan. Then she mixed pancake batter all night long. When she poured the batter in the pan and heard the familiar sizzle, she knew her idea had worked.

3. Roy Campanella was a baseball catcher for the Brooklyn Dodgers. He was named the best player in the National League three times. But his career came to a halt suddenly in 1958 when he was paralyzed in a car wreck.

4. The hare thought he was a pretty fast fellow. One day he thought he would have some fun, so he challenged the tortoise to a race. Much to the hare's delight, the tortoise accepted the challenge. When the day of the race arrived, the hare quickly got ahead and decided to take a nap. The tortoise kept up a slow, steady pace and soon passed the sleeping hare. By the time the hare woke up, it was too late, for the steady tortoise had won the race.

5. John Wesley Powell loved the American West. He liked to study its different rocks and their forms. In 1871, when he was exploring the Colorado River, he found an enormous canyon. It was later named the Grand Canyon. Powell and his group then followed the river through the canyon. They became the first people to go by boat through the Grand Canyon.

Fact	Inference		
○	○	**1.**	**A.** John Milton was a poet.
○	○		**B.** Milton's daughter was very helpful.
○	○		**C.** John Milton went blind.
○	○		**D.** Milton's greatest poem was *Paradise Lost*.

Fact	Inference		
○	○	**2.**	**A.** Mary worked in a cafe.
○	○		**B.** Mary wanted to do something unusual.
○	○		**C.** She cooked the world's largest pancake.
○	○		**D.** The large pancake made Mary famous.

Fact	Inference		
○	○	**3.**	**A.** Roy Campanella was a catcher.
○	○		**B.** The Dodgers played in Brooklyn.
○	○		**C.** Campanella had a car wreck in 1958.
○	○		**D.** His injuries were very serious.

Fact	Inference		
○	○	**4.**	**A.** The hare thought he could beat the tortoise.
○	○		**B.** The race was between the hare and tortoise.
○	○		**C.** The hare underestimated the tortoise.
○	○		**D.** The tortoise won the race.

Fact	Inference		
○	○	**5.**	**A.** Powell explored the Colorado River.
○	○		**B.** Powell found the Grand Canyon.
○	○		**C.** The boat ride in the canyon was exciting.
○	○		**D.** Powell studied rocks and their forms.

1. Janna liked to jog every day. One day as she was jogging, she spotted something in the grass, so she decided to investigate. It was a wallet full of money. Janna knew she could just keep the money, and no one would ever find out about it. But Janna also knew that the person who lost the wallet probably needed the money. So Janna took the wallet to the police station.

2. When Jim Abbott was born, part of his arm had not formed completely. He had only one working hand, but Jim made the most of his situation. In college Jim became the star pitcher of the baseball team. He played so well that he was later signed by a professional team. Jim Abbott became a major league pitcher.

3. In Greek legends King Midas loved gold and wealth. For an act of friendship, Midas received a wish from the gods. Midas wished that everything he touched would turn to gold. The king was granted his wish, but he soon realized he had made a serious mistake when even his food and drink turned to gold.

4. Mosquitoes are a tremendous problem in the summer. Mosquitoes love the hot weather. Then they can fly around and bite as many people as they want. But mosquitoes can't beat their wings in cool weather. The temperature must be more than sixty degrees for mosquitoes to fly.

5. Janet was waiting in line at the supermarket. The line at the checkout counter was long, and some of the customers were getting angry. The clerk was having trouble with the cash register. Janet could see that the clerk was about to cry. Finally Janet's turn came to check out. Janet paid for her purchase and smiled as the clerk returned her change. After counting the change, Janet realized the clerk had given her too much money. Janet informed the clerk, and the clerk smiled in appreciation.

Fact	Inference		
○	○	**1.** A.	Janna was an honest person.
○	○	B.	A wallet was lying in the grass.
○	○	C.	The police found the owner of the wallet.
○	○	D.	Jogging was Janna's favorite activity.

Fact	Inference		
○	○	**2.** A.	Abbott overcame his disability.
○	○	B.	People were impressed by Abbott's skill.
○	○	C.	In college Abbott was a pitcher.
○	○	D.	Abbott was signed by a professional team.

Fact	Inference		
○	○	**3.** A.	King Midas loved gold.
○	○	B.	Everything Midas touched turned to gold.
○	○	C.	King Midas was greedy.
○	○	D.	The king didn't like his golden touch.

Fact	Inference		
○	○	**4.** A.	Mosquitoes love hot weather.
○	○	B.	People are bothered by mosquitoes.
○	○	C.	Mosquitoes' wings don't beat in cool weather.
○	○	D.	Cool weather means fewer mosquito bites.

Fact	Inference		
○	○	**5.** A.	The customers didn't like waiting in line.
○	○	B.	Janet was a good person.
○	○	C.	The clerk was having a bad day.
○	○	D.	Janet received too much change.

1. Tonya didn't know much about soccer, but her friend Sharon convinced her to join the team. Today they were playing their first game. Suddenly Tonya saw the ball coming toward her, so she stopped it with her foot and started kicking it down the field. She couldn't understand why all her teammates were yelling and waving at her. All the people in the stands were laughing. Then Tonya gave the ball a mighty kick and scored in the wrong goal!

2. Alexis Carrel was a famous American doctor. He felt that progress in medicine could make the world a better place. Carrel researched blood for many years. He showed its importance in healing. For his work he won the Nobel Prize for Medicine in 1912. Later he helped invent the mechanical heart.

3. Miguel de Cervantes was a great writer from Spain. His most famous work, *Don Quixote*, was about an old man from La Mancha. Don Quixote imagines himself to be a knight, and he sets out to correct all the wrongs in the world. He does not do well, though, for he cannot tell the real from the unreal. He even attacks a windmill that he mistakes for a giant.

4. Today cameras can be bought and used by almost everyone. This was not always true. The first actual camera was made in 1816. Twenty years later the first permanent photo was made. Next, photos were made on silver plates. But the equipment was costly and heavy. In 1888 the affordable box camera was first sold to the public.

5. W. C. Handy grew up in Alabama. Even as a boy, he liked to make music. As he grew older, he traveled across the country playing in a small band. He began to write songs, mostly about feeling blue, or sad. Handy saw the difficulties of African Americans, and he wrote about them. His songs became hits, and he earned the nickname "Father of the Blues."

Fact	Inference		
○	○	**1.**	**A.** Tonya didn't know much about soccer.
○	○		**B.** Sharon convinced Tonya to join the team.
○	○		**C.** Tonya kicked the ball in the wrong goal.
○	○		**D.** Tonya's mistake made the people laugh.

Fact	Inference		
○	○	**2.**	**A.** Carrel helped invent a mechanical heart.
○	○		**B.** Alexis Carrel wanted to help people.
○	○		**C.** Dr. Carrel won the Nobel Prize.
○	○		**D.** Alexis Carrel was a good doctor.

Fact	Inference		
○	○	**3.**	**A.** Don Quixote attacks a windmill.
○	○		**B.** Cervantes was a Spanish writer.
○	○		**C.** Don Quixote has an active imagination.
○	○		**D.** Cervantes wrote his books in Spanish.

Fact	Inference		
○	○	**4.**	**A.** The box camera made photography popular.
○	○		**B.** Today cameras can be used by almost everyone.
○	○		**C.** The first actual camera was made in 1816.
○	○		**D.** The box camera was first sold in 1888.

Fact	Inference		
○	○	**5.**	**A.** W. C. Handy was an African American.
○	○		**B.** Handy grew up in Alabama.
○	○		**C.** "Father of the Blues" was Handy's nickname.
○	○		**D.** Handy's favorite music was the blues.

1. Delisa had often seen people sleeping on the sidewalks downtown. Usually she didn't think twice about them. But one day she saw a young mother with two small children. They were getting food from a trash can behind a cafe. The sight made Delisa cry, and she promised herself she would do something to help. The next day she began a food drive for the homeless.

2. Bertha von Suttner's life was one of peace and goodwill. As a young woman, she served as the assistant to millionaire Alfred Nobel. Later she married and moved to Paris. Suttner later suggested to Nobel that he start a program to reward people who work for peace. Nobel accepted her plan. Suttner then gave a series of speeches pleading for peace. In 1905 Suttner became the first woman to win the Nobel Peace Prize.

3. In 1963 Ron was in the sixth grade. One cold November day, the principal stepped into the classroom. She quietly told the class that President Kennedy had been shot and killed. The teacher and some of the students began to weep. Ron just stared out the window with a glassy look in his eyes.

4. The history of the world is an endless tale of war. Nations fight for all sorts of reasons. There is almost always a war going on somewhere. Only one continent, Antarctica, has never had a war.

5. In Greek legends Oedipus was once the king of Thebes. But he lost his throne and was forced by the gods to roam the Greek countryside with his daughter, Antigone. Oedipus was a blind, old man when he arrived at the fountain at Colonus. He was tired from his long years of wandering. He tasted the fountain's cool water, and he suddenly felt young again. Oedipus felt that he would be content to die there. Antigone honored her father's wish.

Fact	Inference		
○	○	**1.** **A.**	Delisa felt sorry for homeless people.
○	○	**B.**	The homeless people slept on sidewalks.
○	○	**C.**	A young mother got food from a trash can.
○	○	**D.**	Delisa realized that the homeless need help.

Fact	Inference		
○	○	**2.** **A.**	Alfred Nobel was a millionaire.
○	○	**B.**	Suttner worked for Alfred Nobel.
○	○	**C.**	Nobel thought a peace prize was a good idea.
○	○	**D.**	Suttner won the Nobel Peace Prize.

Fact	Inference		
○	○	**3.** **A.**	Ron was in sixth grade.
○	○	**B.**	The students were upset by the bad news.
○	○	**C.**	Ron was sad to hear about Kennedy's death.
○	○	**D.**	The day in November was cold.

Fact	Inference		
○	○	**4.** **A.**	No wars have been fought in Antarctica.
○	○	**B.**	Soldiers don't like to fight in the cold.
○	○	**C.**	Antarctica has a small population.
○	○	**D.**	There is almost always a war going on.

Fact	Inference		
○	○	**5.** **A.**	Oedipus was once the king of Thebes.
○	○	**B.**	Antigone was the daughter of Oedipus.
○	○	**C.**	Oedipus was old and blind.
○	○	**D.**	Antigone respected her father.

1. The Pig War took place in the 1880s between Great Britain and the United States. It was not really a war, just a big argument. The dispute happened on an island off the state of Washington. An American man shot a pig owned by a British man. Because of this event, the two nations were willing to go to war. But the problem was solved without fighting.

2. As the ants worked to gather food for the winter, the grasshopper enjoyed himself. He played the fiddle and took long naps. The ants warned him that he should get busy, but he ignored them. Soon winter arrived, and the grasshopper found himself hungry and miserable out in the cold.

3. As a child Jane Goodall loved to study animals and insects. She took notes on birds and bugs. She even opened a small museum for her friends. She hoped to travel to Africa when she grew up. At age 23 she got her wish and went to Kenya. She stayed in Africa and has become a famous scientist. Her field of study is the behavior of chimpanzees. Goodall has claimed her success is due to patience, courage, observation, and will power.

4. Salty Sam worked in a silver mine. He always took a canary with him into the mine. The yellow bird furnished him with music as he worked. But he had a better reason for taking the canary along. If the canary stopped singing, Sam knew the air in the mine was almost gone.

5. Richard Byrd was a famous American explorer. In 1930 he was in Antarctica. His party had to leave suddenly because of illness. Byrd returned to his base there three years later. Though the buildings they had used earlier were covered with ice, things inside were exactly as they had left them. A mess on a dining table remained. Food they had left was still good. Even the lights sprang to life after being off for so long.

Fact	Inference		
○	○	**1.**	**A.** The Pig War took place on an island.
○	○		**B.** The man was upset that his pig was shot.
○	○		**C.** An American man shot the pig.
○	○		**D.** The two governments met to discuss the problem.

Fact	Inference		
○	○	**2.**	**A.** The grasshopper would rather play than work.
○	○		**B.** The ants were hard workers.
○	○		**C.** The grasshopper played the fiddle.
○	○		**D.** The ants knew food was scarce in the winter.

Fact	Inference		
○	○	**3.**	**A.** Jane Goodall studies chimpanzees.
○	○		**B.** Her friends liked Goodall's museum.
○	○		**C.** Jane Goodall enjoys her work.
○	○		**D.** Goodall went to Kenya at age 23.

Fact	Inference		
○	○	**4.**	**A.** Salty Sam worked in a silver mine.
○	○		**B.** Sam took a canary with him into the mine.
○	○		**C.** The canary furnished Sam with music.
○	○		**D.** If the bird stopped singing, Sam left the mine.

Fact	Inference		
○	○	**5.**	**A.** Antarctica is cold and icy.
○	○		**B.** Richard Byrd was an American explorer.
○	○		**C.** Richard Byrd was in Antarctica in 1930.
○	○		**D.** The explorers were in a hurry when they left.

1. Louis Armstrong was born in New Orleans, a city known for its music. At age nine Louis was singing for pennies on street corners. Later he moved to New York. In New York he began to play the trumpet, and he became famous across the country. Louis had a unique singing voice that helped to make his songs hits. He became fondly known as "Satchmo."

2. Shirley's baseball team was not very good, and it had not won a game all season. Something had to be done, or else the team would be laughed at by everyone in town. So Shirley promised to eat one bug for every run the team scored. That night the team scored 20 runs and finally won a game.

3. René Réaumur was a well-known French scientist. One day he watched as a wasp constructed its nest. Réaumur noticed that the wasp used wood fibers to build its nest. He realized that the nest felt like paper. His research introduced the use of wood fibers in papermaking.

4. In Greek legends Orpheus was a singer of sweet music. As a young man, he married a beautiful woman named Eurydice. But then she stepped on a poisonous snake and died. Orpheus was filled with grief, and he decided to go to the underworld to win his wife back from death. In the dark caverns below the earth, he charmed Hades, king of the underworld, with his sad song. Hades agreed to release Eurydice on one condition. Orpheus could not look back at her until they reached the earth's surface. Orpheus agreed, and he began to lead his wife from the darkness. But just once, to make sure she was still following, Orpheus looked back. His dear wife vanished instantly.

5. Scientists have studied sleep and dreams. They have found that different kinds of dreams can be caused by the temperature of the bedroom. As the bedroom gets colder, sleepers have more bad dreams.

Fact	Inference		
○	○	**1.** **A.**	Louis Armstrong was born in New Orleans.
○	○	**B.**	"Satchmo" was Armstrong's nickname.
○	○	**C.**	People liked Armstrong's singing voice.
○	○	**D.**	Louis Armstrong played the trumpet.

Fact	Inference		
○	○	**2.** **A.**	Shirley's team was not very good.
○	○	**B.**	The players thought her plan was strange.
○	○	**C.**	Shirley ate 20 bugs after her team won.
○	○	**D.**	Her plan was a success.

Fact	Inference		
○	○	**3.** **A.**	Réaumur was interested in wasps.
○	○	**B.**	René Réaumur was a French scientist.
○	○	**C.**	The wasp used wood fibers to build its nest.
○	○	**D.**	Réaumur learned papermaking after watching the wasp.

Fact	Inference		
○	○	**4.** **A.**	Orpheus was a singer of sweet music.
○	○	**B.**	Eurydice was the wife of Orpheus.
○	○	**C.**	Hades was the king of the underworld.
○	○	**D.**	Orpheus loved his wife very much.

Fact	Inference		
○	○	**5.** **A.**	Uncomfortable conditions cause bad dreams.
○	○	**B.**	Sleepers in cold rooms have more bad dreams.
○	○	**C.**	Some scientists study sleep and dreams.
○	○	**D.**	People tell scientists about their dreams.

1. Tulips were first grown in Turkey. The word *tulip* comes from a Turkish word meaning turban. A turban is a type of scarf worn wrapped around the head. In the 1600s tulips became very popular in Holland. Single tulip bulbs were bought and sold for incredibly high prices.

2. Many breeds of dogs are used for work. In some cultures dogs are used to herd sheep. The dogs keep the flock from being attacked by animals such as wolves. They also keep sheep from wandering off. Sheepdogs are known for their loyalty and gentleness.

3. Brett and Steve were spending a week at camp. Tonight was their last night, and it was "skit night." The campers in each cabin had written plays about their camp experiences. Brett had seen how easily Steve made friends with everyone in the camp. When Steve was chosen to be the announcer for skit night, Brett dumped a box of cookie crumbs in Steve's sleeping bag.

4. In 1826 a French inventor named Joseph Niepce made the first photograph. He coated a metal plate with a special chemical. Then he exposed the plate to light for about eight hours. Thirteen years later British inventor William Fox Talbot introduced the use of negatives. This process allowed many photos to be made from one negative.

5. Kristin and her younger brother Andrew were planning to surprise their parents for their anniversary. They wanted to take them out to a nice French restaurant. After considering several ways to earn money, Kristin had an idea. The next Saturday Kristin and Andrew set up a soft-pretzel and lemonade stand in the park. They sold 57 soft pretzels and 83 cups of lemonade. The money they made was more than enough for their parents' anniversary surprise.

Fact | Inference
| | **1.** **A.** Tulips were popular in Holland.
○ | ○ |
○ | ○ | **B.** Only wealthy people could buy tulips.
○ | ○ | **C.** The word *tulip* comes from a Turkish word.
○ | ○ | **D.** Tulips look similar to turbans.

Fact | Inference
○ | ○ | **2.** **A.** Wolves are afraid of sheepdogs.
○ | ○ | **B.** Sheepdogs are gentle and loyal.
○ | ○ | **C.** There are many breeds of dogs.
○ | ○ | **D.** Sheepdogs are intelligent.

Fact | Inference
○ | ○ | **3.** **A.** Brett was jealous of Steve.
○ | ○ | **B.** Steve made friends easily.
○ | ○ | **C.** Brett and Steve slept in the same cabin.
○ | ○ | **D.** Steve was chosen to be the announcer.

Fact | Inference
○ | ○ | **4.** **A.** Niepce made the first photograph.
○ | ○ | **B.** It was easier to make photos from negatives.
○ | ○ | **C.** Niepce did not use negatives.
○ | ○ | **D.** The metal plate was exposed for eight hours.

Fact | Inference
○ | ○ | **5.** **A.** Andrew is younger than Kristin.
○ | ○ | **B.** Kristin and Andrew like French food.
○ | ○ | **C.** The people at the park were thirsty.
○ | ○ | **D.** Kristin and Andrew sold pretzels.

1. The average weight for male cats is 8.6 pounds. The average for females is 7.2 pounds. The heaviest recorded weight for a cat is nearly 47 pounds. This cat lived in Cairns, Australia, and was named Himmy. Himmy lived to be 10 years old. The average male cat that is well fed and receives good medical care lives about 15 years.

2. Sundials are an ancient way of measuring time. Experts believe they were used by the Babylonians in 2000 B.C. A sundial measures the angle of a shadow cast by the sun. As the sun moves from east to west during the day, so does the shadow. The shadow is cast by a flat piece of metal in the center of the dial. In the Northern Hemisphere, the metal piece must point toward the North Pole.

3. Allison was upset over a difficult homework problem. She had been working on it for a while, but she still couldn't get the answer. "Why don't we go outside for a walk?" her dad suggested. Allison looked up at the stars as they walked. Her dad pointed out the planet Venus. When they returned home, Allison felt ready to tackle the homework problem. "Thanks for the walk, Dad," she said.

4. The first band-aid was created in 1920 by Earle Dickson. He was a cotton buyer for a drug company. The bandage was designed for Dickson's wife, who frequently cut herself while cooking.

5. Scott was tired from jogging, so he sat down on a park bench. He noticed a pair of glasses on the bench. When he asked several people sitting nearby whether the glasses belonged to them, they all said no. Since he couldn't find the owner, Scott decided he would take the glasses home. He put an ad in the lost and found section of the local newspaper.

Fact	Inference		
○	○	**1.**	**A.** Male cats are bigger than females.
○	○		**B.** Himmy weighed nearly 47 pounds.
○	○		**C.** An average male cat weighs 8.6 pounds.
○	○		**D.** Himmy lived to be 10 years old.

Fact	Inference		
○	○	**2.**	**A.** Sundials measure time.
○	○		**B.** The sun moves from east to west.
○	○		**C.** Sundials are useless at night.
○	○		**D.** Time was important to the Babylonians.

Fact	Inference		
○	○	**3.**	**A.** The walk helped Allison calm down.
○	○		**B.** Allison's father wanted to help her.
○	○		**C.** Allison was doing her homework at night.
○	○		**D.** Allison was upset over her homework.

Fact	Inference		
○	○	**4.**	**A.** Dickson's wife frequently cut herself.
○	○		**B.** Band-aids were created in 1920.
○	○		**C.** Dickson worked for a drug company.
○	○		**D.** Dickson was concerned about his wife.

Fact	Inference		
○	○	**5.**	**A.** Scott was tired from jogging.
○	○		**B.** Scott is a responsible person.
○	○		**C.** The glasses were on the bench.
○	○		**D.** Scott placed an ad in the paper.

1. Dragons aren't just creatures found in fairy tales. Komodo dragons are 10-foot-long lizards. They are found on the island of Komodo and other small islands in Indonesia. They have long tails and are covered with small scales. The open mouth of a Komodo dragon reveals rows of teeth that look like the edge of a saw.

2. The big homecoming dance was Friday night, and Suzanne needed a dress to wear. As she was sorting through her closet, her older sister Jean tapped her on the shoulder. She knew that Suzanne had always liked her blue dress. "How would you like to wear this?" she asked. Suzanne's eyes lit up. She hugged Jean and ran to try on the dress.

3. It was Wednesday afternoon, and Jim's book report was due Thursday morning. The book he had checked out at the library sat untouched in the same spot where it had been for the last 14 days. Suddenly an idea came to Jim. He remembered that his older sister kept her papers from last year's class in a notebook in her closet.

4. Stonehenge is a circle of huge stones on the Salisbury Plain in England. The average weight of each stone is 28 tons. The monument was probably built between 2800 and 2000 B.C., but no one knows who placed the stones there or what their exact purpose was. Placement of the stones made it possible to predict sunrises and sunsets, changes in the seasons, and even eclipses of the sun and moon.

5. The sun was just beginning to peek through the pine trees when Marisa opened her eyes. She had slept soundly in her sleeping bag all through the night. The birds sang as she got up, packed her heavy backpack, and continued the hike with the rest of her family. After two hours of steep, uphill hiking, they reached the top of the mountain. Marisa took off her backpack and sat down to smell the clean air and enjoy the view.

Fact	Inference			
○	○	**1.**	**A.**	Komodo dragons don't live in the United States.
○	○		**B.**	Komodo dragons have scales.
○	○		**C.**	Komodo dragons live on islands.
○	○		**D.**	Komodo dragons look very scary.

Fact	Inference			
○	○	**2.**	**A.**	Jean was kind to her sister.
○	○		**B.**	Suzanne was excited about wearing the dress.
○	○		**C.**	The dance was Friday night.
○	○		**D.**	Jean is older than Suzanne.

Fact	Inference			
○	○	**3.**	**A.**	Jim decided to copy his sister's book report.
○	○		**B.**	His sister is one year older than Jim.
○	○		**C.**	Jim didn't want to read the book.
○	○		**D.**	The book report was due Thursday.

Fact	Inference			
○	○	**4.**	**A.**	Stonehenge is in England.
○	○		**B.**	No one is sure of Stonehenge's purpose.
○	○		**C.**	Each stone weighs about 28 tons.
○	○		**D.**	Eclipses were important to ancient people.

Fact	Inference			
○	○	**5.**	**A.**	Marisa slept soundly.
○	○		**B.**	Marisa's family was on vacation.
○	○		**C.**	Marisa's backpack was heavy.
○	○		**D.**	Marisa enjoys hiking.

1. A limousine is a large luxury car. Most limousines are custom-made. The longest limousine is called "The American Dream." It is sixty feet long, has two engines, and needs two people to drive it. One person drives from the front, and the other drives from the back. The two drivers use headphones to communicate with each other.

2. Bill loved to explore the forest near his house. He stopped for a while to throw stones into the lake. Then he decided to hike deeper into the woods. After over an hour of hiking, he stopped to rest. When it was time to go home, he realized he was unsure of which direction to go.

3. Mount Vesuvius erupted in A.D. 79. It buried the ancient city of Pompeii for hundreds of years. Pompeii was a Roman port that was also an important center of business. Wealthy landowners, shopkeepers, merchants, manufacturers, and slaves lived in Pompeii. Today more than half of Pompeii has been uncovered, and visitors can get a glimpse of what life was like in ancient Rome.

4. Ramón smelled the flowers he had brought with him to the tutoring session. He quickly hid them behind his back when Mrs. Jenkins came into the room. Mrs. Jenkins had been tutoring him in English for the past year, and today was the last session. As Mrs. Jenkins sat down, Ramón surprised her with the bouquet.

5. Anna had stayed up late on Thursday night to finish her model of a volcano for the science fair at school. The next morning she was late for school and did not have time to carefully pack her science project. As she started to dash across the crosswalk in front of the school, she had to stop suddenly to avoid a car she had not seen. "Oh, no!" cried Anna. "Look at my science project!"

Fact	Inference		
○	○	**1. A.**	A limousine is a car.
○	○	**B.**	"The American Dream" needs two drivers.
○	○	**C.**	It is difficult to drive "The American Dream."
○	○	**D.**	"The American Dream" has two engines.

Fact	Inference		
○	○	**2. A.**	Bill is adventurous.
○	○	**B.**	The forest is near Bill's house.
○	○	**C.**	Bill threw stones into the lake.
○	○	**D.**	Bill was tired after hiking.

Fact	Inference		
○	○	**3. A.**	Mount Vesuvius erupted in A.D. 79.
○	○	**B.**	Pompeii was buried for hundreds of years.
○	○	**C.**	Slavery was allowed in Pompeii.
○	○	**D.**	Pompeii was a large city.

Fact	Inference		
○	○	**4. A.**	Ramón wanted to thank Mrs. Jenkins.
○	○	**B.**	Mrs. Jenkins was Ramón's tutor.
○	○	**C.**	Ramón is thoughtful.
○	○	**D.**	Mrs. Jenkins did not expect the flowers.

Fact	Inference		
○	○	**5. A.**	Anna made a model volcano.
○	○	**B.**	On Friday Anna overslept.
○	○	**C.**	Anna dropped her science project.
○	○	**D.**	Anna was late for school.

1. "Be home for dinner by five-thirty," Barb's mother reminded her as Barb walked out the door. "Yes, Mom," Barb answered. After school Barb walked home with her friend Tracy. After having a snack, they went up to Tracy's room. They listened to a tape that Tracy had gotten for her birthday. At six o'clock Barb's mother called Tracy's house to ask if Barb was still there.

2. An eagle soared high above its hunting grounds, carefully watching the ground below. It spotted a chipmunk and swooped down skillfully. The wind whistled through its feathers. At the last second, the chipmunk swerved and escaped harm.

3. One afternoon Pam was buying a loaf of bread for her mother. Pam noticed Samantha in the magazine section of the store. She was about to go over to say hello when she saw Samantha slip one of the magazines under her coat. As Pam gasped in surprise, Samantha looked up and then ran out of the store.

4. Several United States presidents have had disabilities. Theodore Roosevelt was blind in one eye, the result of his having been struck during a boxing match. John Quincy Adams's right arm was smaller than his left arm because of a childhood accident. During his presidency Ronald Reagan wore a hearing aid in both ears to improve his hearing.

5. Everyone had liked Tony since he moved to town. Even the teachers at Lincoln Junior High thought Tony was a nice guy. Because of his popularity, Tony was asked to run for student council president against Holly. Both Tony and Holly put up banners about the election around the school. The day after Tony won the election, Holly ripped up all of Tony's signs.

Fact	Inference		
○	○	**1.** **A.**	Tracy lives near Barb's house.
○	○	**B.**	Barb's mother was worried.
○	○	**C.**	Tracy and Barb are friends.
○	○	**D.**	Barb's mother called Tracy's house.

Fact	Inference		
○	○	**2.** **A.**	The eagle flew high above the ground.
○	○	**B.**	The chipmunk escaped.
○	○	**C.**	Eagles have good eyesight.
○	○	**D.**	Chipmunks are fast.

Fact	Inference		
○	○	**3.** **A.**	Pam went to buy bread.
○	○	**B.**	Samantha was dishonest.
○	○	**C.**	Pam saw what Samantha did.
○	○	**D.**	Samantha was afraid Pam would tell.

Fact	Inference		
○	○	**4.** **A.**	Several presidents have had disabilities.
○	○	**B.**	Reagan wore hearing aids.
○	○	**C.**	These men were successful people.
○	○	**D.**	Adams injured his arm.

Fact	Inference		
○	○	**5.** **A.**	Tony won the election.
○	○	**B.**	Holly put up banners.
○	○	**C.**	Tony made friends easily.
○	○	**D.**	Holly was upset over losing.

1.   Booker T. Washington was born a slave. When all the slaves were freed after the Civil War, he found work as a coal miner. He later attended a trade school for African Americans. In 1879 he became a teacher at this school. Two years later he founded Tuskegee Institute. The school helped students prepare for jobs. Washington believed that by developing strong work skills, African Americans would succeed.

2.   Charlotte admired her mother's pearl ring. One morning she decided she would wear it, without her mother's permission. She dropped it in her purse and decided she would put it on at school. Later she remembered the ring. When she reached into her purse, it was not there.

3.   In 1347 King Tut became king of Egypt. He was only nine years old. Howard Carter discovered Tut's tomb in 1922. He had been searching for it about ten years. The four-room tomb contained over five thousand articles. Many of them were beautifully carved and covered with gold.

4.   Joan was attending a concert with her parents. After the first few minutes, she noticed an odd smell. She whispered to her parents about it. Her parents realized that there was a gas leak in the building. They calmly alerted the ushers. Joan noticed a woman starting to faint as one of the ushers stepped up to the microphone to make an announcement.

5.   Hsing-Hsing and Ling-Ling are giant pandas at the National Zoo in Washington, D.C. Both animals get fan mail, especially when one of them is sick. Sometimes they are even invited to visit homes or classrooms. But the keepers don't let the pandas out of the zoo. However, their keepers do read the mail and occasionally display it at the zoo.

Fact   Inference
○   ○   **1.** **A.** Washington was a hard worker.
○   ○   **B.** Washington was a former slave.
○   ○   **C.** Washington was once a teacher.
○   ○   **D.** Washington cared about his students' future.

Fact   Inference
○   ○   **2.** **A.** Charlotte admired the pearl ring.
○   ○   **B.** Charlotte's mother was angry.
○   ○   **C.** Charlotte took the ring to school.
○   ○   **D.** The ring was not in her purse.

Fact   Inference
○   ○   **3.** **A.** Carter searched for the tomb about ten years.
○   ○   **B.** King Tut was loved by his people.
○   ○   **C.** The tomb was discovered in 1922.
○   ○   **D.** King Tut was king of Egypt.

Fact   Inference
○   ○   **4.** **A.** Joan is very observant.
○   ○   **B.** A woman started to faint.
○   ○   **C.** Joan's parents like concerts.
○   ○   **D.** An usher told the audience to exit.

Fact   Inference
○   ○   **5.** **A.** The pandas are famous.
○   ○   **B.** People send mail to the pandas.
○   ○   **C.** The keepers read the fan mail.
○   ○   **D.** The pandas are invited to visit schools.

1. Paul and Jack needed to earn points for a merit badge. Jack's mother worked at a nursing home and suggested they volunteer their time. The boys called the activities director at the nursing home. They asked how they could help. The following Saturday the boys helped the residents on a shopping trip to the mall.

2. Redwoods are among the tallest trees in the world. Some redwoods have trunks that are 8 to 12 feet across. One redwood in northern California is the tallest known tree in the world. It is 368 feet high. The trees tend to grow very close to each other. This shuts out the sunlight below. For that reason there are few plants that grow around the redwoods.

3. Whenever Celeste visited her mother's office, she was bothered by the number of aluminum cans she saw in the trash. She asked her mother if she could help recycle the cans. The next day Celeste found a large box. Then she made a sign that said "Aluminum Cans Only."

4. As a child Florence Nightingale enjoyed playing nurse to her dolls and once saved the life of a dog. Although her family was wealthy, she rejected British society. She preferred instead to be a nurse. In 1854 she was asked to help wounded British troops who were fighting the Crimean War. Today she is considered the founder of the nursing profession.

5. Wallace had a bad habit of leaving books, hats, shoes, and almost anything on the stairs. His mother and father constantly reminded Wallace to pick up his things on the stairs. One night around midnight, Wallace's father decided to go downstairs for a snack. He didn't want to disturb the family, so he didn't turn on the lights.

Fact	Inference		
○	○	**1.**	**A.** The boys asked how they could help.
○	○		**B.** Jack's mother works at a nursing home.
○	○		**C.** The boys went shopping with the residents.
○	○		**D.** Paul and Jack are kind.

Fact	Inference		
○	○	**2.**	**A.** Redwoods block out the sunlight.
○	○		**B.** Redwoods grow mostly in California.
○	○		**C.** Redwoods grow close together.
○	○		**D.** Plants need light to grow.

Fact	Inference		
○	○	**3.**	**A.** Celeste's mother works in an office.
○	○		**B.** Celeste cares about the environment.
○	○		**C.** Celeste's mother took the sign to work.
○	○		**D.** Celeste found a box.

Fact	Inference		
○	○	**4.**	**A.** Nightingale was a nurse.
○	○		**B.** Nightingale's family was wealthy.
○	○		**C.** Nightingale wanted to help people.
○	○		**D.** Nightingale liked animals.

Fact	Inference		
○	○	**5.**	**A.** Wallace was forgetful.
○	○		**B.** Wallace left his things on the stairs.
○	○		**C.** Wallace's father tripped down the stairs.
○	○		**D.** Wallace's father didn't turn on the lights.

1. Lewis Lyons was the youngest artist ever to show his work at England's Royal Academy of Arts. He painted *Trees and Monkeys* when he was only three years old. The academy showed the work in 1967.

2. Kay threw her bike down wherever she stopped. More than once she had left her bicycle in the driveway. Several times her dad had pointed out what could happen when she did this. One morning as her dad was leaving for work, Kay heard a crashing sound outside.

3. Polio was once one of the most dreaded diseases in the United States. But in 1955 Jonas E. Salk helped change that. His polio vaccine was given to thousands of schoolchildren in Pittsburgh. Not one of the children came down with a case of polio. Soon afterwards the entire country was urged to have polio vaccinations.

4. Lou Ann and her mother were driving home one evening. They had been visiting Lou Ann's aunt. Lou Ann soon noticed that her mother was slowing down. Fog had blanketed the highway, and it was getting almost impossible to see the road. For the next hour, their car crept slowly along the road. When they finally reached home safely, Lou Ann and her mother hugged each other.

5. Chuck looked at the scoreboard as he walked up to bat. The game was tied 13 to 13. His teammates Perry and Roberto had struck out before him. With the bases loaded, the pitcher threw a curve ball to Chuck. Swinging as hard as he could, Chuck felt the ball hit squarely on the bat.

Fact	Inference		
○	○	**1.** **A.**	Lyons was interested in monkeys.
○	○	**B.**	Lyons' work was shown in 1967.
○	○	**C.**	Lyons was a good artist.
○	○	**D.**	Lyons painted *Trees and Monkeys*.

Fact	Inference		
○	○	**2.** **A.**	Kay didn't put her bike away.
○	○	**B.**	Her dad ran over Kay's bike.
○	○	**C.**	Kay rode her bike often.
○	○	**D.**	Kay learned a lesson from her mistake.

Fact	Inference		
○	○	**3.** **A.**	Polio is a disease.
○	○	**B.**	Salk's vaccine saved many people.
○	○	**C.**	The vaccine was given to children.
○	○	**D.**	Salk's vaccine was an important discovery.

Fact	Inference		
○	○	**4.** **A.**	Lou Ann's mother is a cautious driver.
○	○	**B.**	Lou Ann was relieved to get home.
○	○	**C.**	The highway was foggy.
○	○	**D.**	Lou Ann's mother slowed down.

Fact	Inference		
○	○	**5.** **A.**	Chuck's team won the game.
○	○	**B.**	The pitcher threw a curve ball.
○	○	**C.**	The game was tied.
○	○	**D.**	Perry had struck out.

1. Matt was playing ball in the back yard when his sister burst from the house. "Chris has a piece of candy stuck in her throat and can't breathe!" she shouted. Matt quickly ran inside and found Chris lying on the floor. She was turning blue. Remembering some of his first-aid training, Matt picked up Chris and wrapped his arms just below her chest. He pushed in and up three times. Suddenly Chris started to cry.

2. In the years before the American Civil War, there was a federal law that allowed slave owners to reclaim their escaped slaves. Anthony Burns was born a slave in Virginia. He escaped to Boston in 1854. He lived and worked there for a few months before his former owner appeared and had him arrested. The trial of Anthony Burns triggered angry mobs in Boston, a city where most people were against slavery. He was forced to go back to Virginia with his master, but he later gained his freedom.

3. In 1911 Hiram Bingham made the greatest archeological discovery that has ever been made in the Americas. The Incas were people who lived in Peru many years ago. Bingham was fascinated with them and dreamed of uncovering one of their lost cities. High in the mountains of Peru he found Machu Picchu. It was an abandoned Inca city. In 1948 Bingham was the guest of honor at a celebration of the Peruvian government's opening of a road to Machu Picchu.

4. May's parents were having guests for dinner. Her mother asked May to help set the table. She noticed that May was trying to carry too many dishes at a time. She warned her, but May paid no attention. May loaded down a tray with ten crystal glasses and had trouble lifting the heavy tray.

5. People sometimes get hiccups after eating rapidly. But for Charles Osborne of Anthon, Iowa, his hiccups began when he was butchering a hog. Unable to find a cure, he continued to hiccup several times a minute for 67 years.

Fact	Inference			
○	○	**1.**	**A.**	Matt used his first-aid training.
○	○		**B.**	A piece of candy was stuck in Chris's throat.
○	○		**C.**	Matt saved Chris's life.
○	○		**D.**	Matt stayed calm in an emergency.

Fact	Inference			
○	○	**2.**	**A.**	Burns escaped to Boston.
○	○		**B.**	Burns was forced to return to slavery.
○	○		**C.**	People in Boston did not own slaves.
○	○		**D.**	Burns was arrested.

Fact	Inference			
○	○	**3.**	**A.**	Machu Picchu was an Inca city.
○	○		**B.**	Bingham was an archeologist.
○	○		**C.**	Machu Picchu was found in 1911.
○	○		**D.**	Bingham returned to Peru in 1948.

Fact	Inference			
○	○	**4.**	**A.**	May didn't pay attention to her mother.
○	○		**B.**	The tray was heavy.
○	○		**C.**	May dropped the tray.
○	○		**D.**	May's parents were having guests.

Fact	Inference			
○	○	**5.**	**A.**	Osborne was from Iowa.
○	○		**B.**	Osborne was a farmer.
○	○		**C.**	Osborne did not find a cure for his hiccups.
○	○		**D.**	Osborne's hiccups lasted 67 years.

1. Most people's sleep follows a definite pattern. In stage one the body starts to relax. In stage two brain waves become slower. As the body approaches stage three, it enters deep sleep. It is not easy to be awakened at this stage. When a person is in stage four, it is even more difficult to be awakened. This is when some people walk or talk in their sleep.

2. High school had not been easy for Diane. Her friends seemed to have so much more time for fun than she did. But today was special. As she walked up the steps in her black cap and gown, she felt a real sense of pride. Glancing over at her parents, she saw her mother wipe a tear from her cheek.

3. Robert E. Peary led an expedition to the North Pole in 1909. His assistant, Matthew Henson, was the only American who accompanied him. Henson, an African American, worked as Peary's personal assistant for more than twenty years. During the trip Peary became ill and had to stop. He urged Henson to complete the journey.

4. Orson Welles' radio broadcast of *War of the Worlds* in 1938 was intended as a special Halloween program. It was a story about Martians attacking Earth. Thousands of listeners took the broadcast seriously. Many in the New York and New Jersey area got in their cars to escape what they thought was a Martian attack. The morning after the broadcast, Welles denied that he or anyone else at the radio station knew about the panic.

5. To Sheila the alarm clock seemed to go off especially early that morning. She forced herself out of bed and started putting on her running clothes. Once she was outside, the cold air helped her wake up. It was just a few days before the race, and she wanted to be in top condition.

Fact	Inference		
○	○	**1.** **A.**	Sleep follows a pattern.
○	○	**B.**	People talk in their sleep in stage four.
○	○	**C.**	Scientists have learned a lot about sleep.
○	○	**D.**	It is hard to wake up in stage three.

Fact	Inference		
○	○	**2.** **A.**	Diane spent a lot of time studying.
○	○	**B.**	Her parents were proud of Diane.
○	○	**C.**	It was graduation day.
○	○	**D.**	Diane felt a sense of pride.

Fact	Inference		
○	○	**3.** **A.**	Henson was an African American.
○	○	**B.**	Peary was an American.
○	○	**C.**	Henson was dedicated.
○	○	**D.**	Henson reached the North Pole.

Fact	Inference		
○	○	**4.** **A.**	Welles broadcasted a Halloween program.
○	○	**B.**	People took the show seriously.
○	○	**C.**	Radio was popular in 1938.
○	○	**D.**	People in New Jersey tried to escape.

Fact	Inference		
○	○	**5.** **A.**	Sheila enjoys running.
○	○	**B.**	The alarm clock seemed to go off early.
○	○	**C.**	The cold air helped Sheila wake up.
○	○	**D.**	It was a few days before the race.

1. Twenty thousand years ago, ice sheets covered much of the western United States, all of New England, and most of Canada. About ten thousand years ago, the ice began to melt. As the ice melted, it began to move. Moving sheets of ice are called glaciers. Most glaciers move very slowly, usually less than two feet a day. As the glaciers moved, they cut valleys through the land and made rolling hills.

2. It was Jonathan's first day at his new school. Before school, groups of students gathered in front of the building. It seemed as if everyone but Jonathan was with a group of friends. They were all talking and laughing together. He walked over to a bench and sat down to read. Then he noticed someone coming toward him. It was Paul, a boy he had met last summer at the pool.

3. Training for the Olympics takes a lot of time. Most Olympic athletes don't get the chance to meet other Olympians. But that's not the case with Jackie Joyner-Kersee. She and her sister-in-law, Florence Griffith Joyner (also known as Flo-Jo), are both world-class athletes. In the 1988 Summer Olympics in Seoul, Korea, Joyner-Kersee set an Olympic record in the long jump. Flo-Jo set a new world record in the 200-meter dash and an Olympic record in the 100-meter dash.

4. Nick overheard a conversation between Colleen and a friend. He thought he heard Colleen tell her friend that she was failing math. Nick told some of his friends what he thought he had heard. The next day Colleen saw Nick in the hall at school. Nick noticed that Colleen's eyes looked red.

5. The copier is not an invention of the twentieth century. When Thomas Jefferson retired from the presidency, he used a copying machine called a polygraph. He used the polygraph to make file copies of the many letters he wrote to people in all parts of the world.

Fact	Inference		
○	○	**1.**	**A.** Glaciers are moving sheets of ice.
○	○		**B.** Today the land in New England is hilly.
○	○		**C.** Glaciers made rolling hills.
○	○		**D.** About ten thousand years ago, the earth became warmer.

Fact	Inference		
○	○	**2.**	**A.** Jonathan was new to the school.
○	○		**B.** The students were talking outside.
○	○		**C.** Jonathan felt lonely.
○	○		**D.** Jonathan was glad to see Paul.

Fact	Inference		
○	○	**3.**	**A.** The two women are sisters-in-law.
○	○		**B.** The 1988 Summer Olympic games were held in Korea.
○	○		**C.** Flo-Jo trained hard for the Olympics.
○	○		**D.** Both women set Olympic records.

Fact	Inference		
○	○	**4.**	**A.** Colleen and Nick are in the same grade.
○	○		**B.** Nick likes to spread gossip.
○	○		**C.** Colleen had been crying.
○	○		**D.** Nick overheard a conversation.

Fact	Inference		
○	○	**5.**	**A.** Jefferson wrote a lot of letters.
○	○		**B.** A polygraph is a copying machine.
○	○		**C.** Jefferson had friends all over the world.
○	○		**D.** Jefferson used the polygraph to copy letters.

1. An animal's eyeshine color is the color that reflects from the back surface of the eye. This reflection increases the animal's night vision ability. An animal's eyeshine color helps to identify the animal. For example the eyeshine color of cats and bullfrogs is green. The eyeshine color of an alligator is ruby red.

2. Hope and Dave were playing a game of checkers. Their parents were out for the evening. The wind had been howling for the past several minutes. Then Hope and Dave heard the tornado siren go off. But before they could scramble down the basement stairs, the lights went out. The next thing Dave knew, his sister was screaming. She was trapped by a large beam that had fallen from the ceiling.

3. The *Atocha* was the flagship of a fleet of Spanish ships. The fleet sailed from Cuba in 1611. It was carrying 47 tons of gold and silver back to Spain. But a powerful hurricane sank the ship. Divers were sent to recover the great treasure. But they found only the ship's two bronze cannons. More than two hundred years later, Mel Fisher found the *Atocha*. He had been searching for it for 19 years.

4. Pat couldn't get the awful conversation out of her mind. She had been so angry with Kate that she had said some things she didn't really mean. Now she wished she had put a big piece of tape over her mouth. Then she noticed the telephone on the kitchen wall. She grabbed the receiver and started to dial.

5. The campfire flames danced toward the sky. The crackling fire sounded warm and familiar to Tom, like the fire in his grandparents' fireplace. Tom leaned back and thought about what a great day it had been. It felt good to relax.

Fact	Inference		
○	○	**1.**	**A.** Animals that are out at night have eyeshine.
○	○		**B.** Eyeshine colors can identify animals.
○	○		**C.** An alligator's eyeshine color is red.
○	○		**D.** Eyeshine increases an animal's night vision.

Fact	Inference		
○	○	**2.**	**A.** A tornado hit the house.
○	○		**B.** Hope and Dave heard the siren.
○	○		**C.** The tornado knocked out the lights.
○	○		**D.** Hope was trapped.

Fact	Inference		
○	○	**3.**	**A.** The *Atocha* carried gold and silver.
○	○		**B.** Fisher found the *Atocha*.
○	○		**C.** A hurricane sank the *Atocha*.
○	○		**D.** Fisher was interested in sunken treasure.

Fact	Inference		
○	○	**4.**	**A.** Pat has a short temper.
○	○		**B.** Pat wanted to apologize to Kate.
○	○		**C.** Pat had gotten angry at Kate.
○	○		**D.** Pat decided to call Kate.

Fact	Inference		
○	○	**5.**	**A.** Tom was sitting near the campfire.
○	○		**B.** It was a cool evening.
○	○		**C.** Tom likes to visit his grandparents.
○	○		**D.** The fire was crackling.

1. "I'll race you to my house!" Meg shouted. Jane struggled to catch up with her. She ran through the deep snow. Both girls dragged their sleds behind them. As soon as they reached the house, they pulled off their wet mittens, scarves, caps, boots, and coats. Meg made hot chocolate and offered some to Jane.

2. Sacagawea was an interpreter and guide for the Lewis and Clark Expedition in the 1800s. She was born a Shoshoni but had been captured by another tribe. She knew several Native American languages and much about the geography of the area.

3. Every time Brian went by the stretch of highway near the shopping mall, he noticed how littered it was. One Saturday he decided to improve the situation. He called some of his friends and told them to meet at his house. Together they walked along the highway, collecting the litter in trash bags.

4. Of the 9 planets in our solar system, Jupiter is the largest. Jupiter spins faster than any other planet. It completes one spin in about 10 hours. The rapid spinning causes it to bulge at its equator and flatten at its poles. Even though its days are shorter than days on Earth, its years are not. It takes about 12 Earth years for Jupiter to complete its journey around the sun.

5. Eleanor Roosevelt was probably the most active first lady in American history. During World War II, she traveled to many parts of the world. After the war she served as United States representative to the United Nations, an organization that promotes peace and international cooperation.

Fact	Inference		
○	○	**1.**	**A.** It was winter.
○	○		**B.** Meg dragged her sled behind her.
○	○		**C.** Jane and Meg are neighbors.
○	○		**D.** Meg offered Jane some hot chocolate.

Fact	Inference		
○	○	**2.**	**A.** Sacagawea spoke several languages.
○	○		**B.** Lewis and Clark were explorers.
○	○		**C.** Sacagawea was an excellent guide.
○	○		**D.** Sacagawea was a Shoshoni.

Fact	Inference		
○	○	**3.**	**A.** Brian was bothered by the litter.
○	○		**B.** Brian's friends were eager to help.
○	○		**C.** Brian called his friends.
○	○		**D.** The boys picked up the litter.

Fact	Inference		
○	○	**4.**	**A.** Jupiter is the largest planet.
○	○		**B.** Jupiter spins faster than any other planet.
○	○		**C.** Jupiter's days are shorter than Earth's.
○	○		**D.** Jupiter is very far away from the sun.

Fact	Inference		
○	○	**5.**	**A.** Roosevelt was an active first lady.
○	○		**B.** The United Nations promotes peace.
○	○		**C.** Roosevelt was interested in world affairs.
○	○		**D.** Roosevelt worked hard for peace.

Think and Apply

One More Step

Read the first two sentences in each item. Then decide what will happen next. Write your answer for each item on the line below the sentences. The first one is done for you.

1. A baby bird was born in the nest its mother built.
When it was full grown, its wings were very strong.

<u>It flew away from the nest.</u>

2. Manuel dumped the dirty laundry into the washer.
He put the laundry in the dryer.

_____

3. Olivia rode her bike to the library.
She found a book she wanted to read.

_____

4. Dad put some water in a pot on the stove.
He turned the burner on high.

_____

5. Jacquelyn finished eating dinner.
She cleared the dishes from the table.

_____

6. The family turned on the television.
A sudden storm knocked down the power lines.

_____

7. Mary wrote the address on the sealed envelope.
She put a stamp in the upper right corner.

_____

Preserving Inferences

Read the paragraph below. Then use the information to infer the answer to each question.

Paul used to work in an office, but now he works at an animal preserve. Many animals at the preserve are from zoos that have closed, but others were born in the wild and have lost their mothers. Most of the animals do not remain at the preserve for very long. Paul knows that he must work hard to prepare the animals for their future. He makes sure all of the animals at the preserve are healthy. He talks to them and handles them with great care. Paul spends hours teaching the animals how to hunt for their own food. He also helps them learn to protect themselves against enemies.

1. Why did Paul decide to work at an animal preserve?

_____

2. What happens to the animals when they leave the preserve?

_____

3. What kind of person is Paul?

_____

4. How does Paul feel about his work?

_____

To check your answers, turn to page 62.

Questions to Ponder

Read each story. Then read the question about the story. Write your answers on the line below each question.

1. Ginger is a horseback-riding teacher. She works with children who have physical disabilities. For the last twenty years, she has been helping her students learn more about themselves while they are learning to ride. At the end of each lesson, Ginger's students leave feeling proud and confident.

   What kind of person is Ginger?

   _____

2. Leroy fed his kitten some cat food and a bowl of milk. When the kitten finished eating, it climbed up in Leroy's lap. The kitten purred as Leroy stroked its fur. Within a few minutes, the little kitten was fast asleep.

   How did the kitten feel when it was in Leroy's lap?

   _____

3. Greg started to cook dinner. He turned on the oven and slid in the casserole. The food would be done in thirty minutes, so he checked his watch to see what time that would be. Just then the telephone rang, and Greg answered it. He spent nearly an hour talking with an old friend.

   What happened to the food in the oven?

   _____

To check your answers, turn to page 62.

Check Yourself

Unit 1 pp. 6-7	Unit 2 pp. 8-9	Unit 3 pp. 10-11	Unit 4 pp. 12-13	Unit 5 pp. 14-15	Unit 6 pp. 16-17	Unit 7 pp. 18-19	Unit 8 pp. 20-21
1.	**1.**	**1.**	**1.**	**1.**	**1.**	**1.**	**1.**
A. I	A. I	A. I	A. F	A. F	A. F	A. F	A. I
B. F	B. F	B. I	B. I	B. F	B. F	B. I	B. F
C. F	C. F	C. F	C. I	C. I	C. I	C. F	C. I
D. I	D. I	D. F	D. I	D. I	D. F	D. F	D. I
2.	**2.**	**2.**	**2.**	**2.**	**2.**	**2.**	**2.**
A. I	A. I	A. F	A. F	A. F	A. F	A. F	A. I
B. I	B. I	B. F	B. I	B. I	B. I	B. I	B. I
C. I	C. I	C. I	C. F	C. I	C. I	C. I	C. F
D. F	D. F	D. F	D. F	D. I	D. F	D. I	D. F
3.	**3.**	**3.**	**3.**	**3.**	**3.**	**3.**	**3.**
A. I	A. F	A. F	A. F	A. F	A. I	A. F	A. F
B. F	B. I	B. I	B. F	B. F	B. F	B. I	B. F
C. I	C. I	C. I	C. I	C. F	C. I	C. F	C. I
D. F	D. I	D. I	D. F	D. I	D. I	D. I	D. I
4.	**4.**	**4.**	**4.**	**4.**	**4.**	**4.**	**4.**
A. I	A. I	A. I	A. I	A. F	A. I	A. I	A. F
B. I	B. F	B. I	B. F	B. F	B. F	B. F	B. I
C. F	C. F	C. F	C. I	C. I	C. I	C. I	C. F
D. F	D. F	D. F	D. I	D. F	D. F	D. F	D. I
5.	**5.**	**5.**	**5.**	**5.**	**5.**	**5.**	**5.**
A. F	A. F	A. F	A. I	A. F	A. F	A. F	A. I
B. F	B. F	B. I	B. F	B. I	B. I	B. F	B. I
C. I	C. I	C. F	C. F	C. F	C. F	C. I	C. I
D. I	D. F	D. F	D. I	D. I	D. I	D. F	D. F

	Unit 9 pp. 22-23	Unit 10 pp. 24-25	Unit 11 pp. 26-27	Unit 12 pp. 28-29	Unit 13 pp. 30-31	Unit 14 pp. 32-33	Unit 15 pp. 34-35	Unit 16 pp. 36-37
1.								
A.	F	I	F	F	F	I	I	F
B.	F	F	I	F	I	F	F	F
C.	F	F	F	I	F	F	F	I
D.	I	I	I	F	I	F	I	F
2.								
A.	F	F	I	F	I	F	I	I
B.	I	F	I	I	F	F	I	F
C.	F	I	F	I	F	I	F	F
D.	I	F	I	I	I	I	F	I
3.								
A.	F	F	F	I	I	I	I	F
B.	F	I	I	F	F	I	I	F
C.	I	I	I	F	I	I	I	I
D.	I	F	F	I	F	F	F	I
4.								
A.	I	F	F	F	F	F	F	I
B.	F	I	F	F	I	F	F	F
C.	F	I	F	F	I	F	F	I
D.	F	F	I	I	F	I	I	I
5.								
A.	I	F	I	I	F	F	F	F
B.	F	F	F	F	I	I	I	I
C.	F	F	F	F	I	F	F	I
D.	I	I	I	I	F	F	I	F

Unit 17 pp.38-39	Unit 18 pp. 40-41	Unit 19 pp. 42-43	Unit 20 pp. 44-45	Unit 21 pp. 46-47	Unit 22 pp. 48-49	Unit 23 pp. 50-51	Unit 24 pp. 52-53	Unit 25 pp. 54-55
1.	**1.**	**1.**	**1.**	**1.**	**1.**	**1.**	**1.**	**1.**
A. I	A. I	A. F	A. I	A. F	A. F	A. F	A. I	A. I
B. I	B. F	B. F	B. F	B. F	B. F	B. I	B. F	B. F
C. F	C. F	C. F	C. I	C. I	C. I	C. F	C. F	C. I
D. F	D. I	D. I	D. F	D. I	D. F	D. I	D. F	D. F
2.	**2.**	**2.**	**2.**	**2.**	**2.**	**2.**	**2.**	**2.**
A. F	A. F	A. F	A. I	A. F	A. I	A. F	A. I	A. F
B. F	B. I	B. I	B. I	B. I	B. I	B. F	B. F	B. I
C. I	C. I	C. F	C. I	C. I	C. I	C. I	C. I	C. I
D. I	D. F	D. I	D. I	D. F	D. F	D. I	D. F	D. F
3.	**3.**	**3.**	**3.**	**3.**	**3.**	**3.**	**3.**	**3.**
A. F	A. F	A. F	A. F	A. F	A. F	A. F	A. F	A. I
B. I	B. I	B. I	B. I	B. I	B. I	B. F	B. F	B. I
C. F	C. F	C. I	C. F	C. F	C. I	C. I	C. F	C. F
D. I	D. F	D. F	D. I	D. I	D. I	D. F	D. I	D. F
4.	**4.**	**4.**	**4.**	**4.**	**4.**	**4.**	**4.**	**4.**
A. F	A. I	A. F	A. I	A. F	A. F	A. I	A. I	A. F
B. F	B. F	B. F	B. I	B. F	B. F	B. I	B. I	B. F
C. I	C. I	C. I	C. F	C. I	C. I	C. I	C. F	C. F
D. F	D. I	D. I	D. F	D. F	D. F	D. F	D. I	D. I
5.	**5.**	**5.**	**5.**	**5.**	**5.**	**5.**	**5.**	**5.**
A. F	A. I	A. I	A. I	A. F	A. I	A. F	A. I	A. F
B. F	B. F	B. F	B. F	B. I	B. F	B. F	B. I	B. F
C. I	C. F	C. I	C. F	C. F	C. F	C. I	C. I	C. I
D. I	D. F	D. F	D. F	D. F	D. F	D. F	D. F	D. I

Practice Making Inferences, Page 4

2. A. F
   B. I
   C. I
   D. F

One More Step, Page 56

Possible answers include:

2. Manuel folded the clean laundry and put it away.
3. Olivia checked out the book and took it home.
4. The water started to boil.
5. Jacquelyn washed the dirty dishes.
6. The television suddenly turned off.
7. Mary mailed the envelope.

Preserving Inferences, Page 57

Possible answers include:

1. He likes working with animals. He likes being a part of wildlife conservation.
2. The animals are returned to the wild.
3. Paul is concerned, gentle, patient, and dedicated.
4. Paul enjoys his work and takes his job seriously.

Questions to Ponder, Page 58

Possible answers include:

1. Ginger is caring, dedicated, and helpful.
2. The kitten felt comfortable and drowsy.
3. The food in the oven started to burn.